FACE PAINTING

Karen Harvey

Copyright © QED Publishing 2015

First published in the UK in 2015
by QED Publishing
Part of The Quarto Group
The Old Brewery, 6 Blundell St,
London, N7 9BH
www.qed-publishing.co.uk

A catalogue record for this book is available
from the British Library.

ISBN 978 1 78493 372 2

Printed in China

Designer: Karen Hood
Editor: Carly Madden
Copy editor: Carron Brown
Photography: Michael Wicks
Editorial Director: Victoria Garrard
Art Director: Laura Roberts-Jensen
Associate Publisher: Maxime Boucknooghe
Publisher: Zeta Jones
Models: Barnaby, Caitlin, Henry, Isaac, Kai,
Lexi, Lily-Mai, Maïa, Phoebe, Poppy, Quinn,
Rio, Ruby, Scarlett, Vince, Yusef, Zainab.

NOTE TO ADULTS

Please note that face paints are not usually
recommended for children under three years.
Do not paint anyone with skin problems,
infections, cold sores or eye infections.

 Never use craft paint
or craft glitter. Use only
paint and cosmetic glitter
that have been designed
to be used safely on skin.

At the top of the page for each project you will
find this handy key. It will tell you the level of
difficulty to expect from each project:

QUICK AND SIMPLE
Easy designs with simple
techniques – perfect for
first-time face painters.

IMPROVE YOUR SKILLS
Fairly straightforward
designs to copy, with
a few extra flourishes.

TRICKY AND CREATIVE
Try these designs once
you're confident you've
mastered the basics.

READY FOR A CHALLENGE
More advanced
designs that need
some practice and a
steady hand to master.

MASTERPIECE
Complex designs and
techniques – build up
experience for these.

Contents

Materials and tools

A face painter's kit needs a few special tools. Take a look at these.

TIP
SPONGES CAN BE PLACED IN A NET BAG AFTER USE, READY TO GO INTO THE WASHING MACHINE AT THE END OF THE DAY.

Sponges

Always use a clean sponge for each face for hygiene reasons. **Baby sponges** cut into quarters are all you need for most designs.

One sponge worth buying is a **stipple sponge**, a textured sponge that is dabbed on the skin. It's perfect for beards, snow or underwater faces.

Circular sponges, 'daubers', can be particularly useful for making perfect circles.

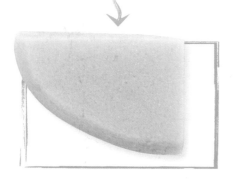

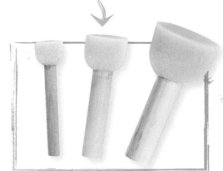

Brushes

Paintbrushes can be bought from art and craft shops, or from face painting retailers. Good quality brushes are important and will help improve your painting. Different-shaped brushes give different results.

The following are good to begin with:

No. 6 round paintbrush

No. 4 round paintbrush

No. 2 round paintbrush

Small filbert brush (curved end)

Large filbert brush (curved end)

Petal brush (fat round brush with a pointed end)

½ inch flat brush

Paints

Face paints are readily available in hobby or craft shops. As you improve, you can experiment to find out which brands of paints are better for certain techniques.

The basic colours you will need for all the faces in this book are:

PAINTS COME IN **FLAT** COLOURS OR **PEARL** COLOURS (SHINY).

Yellow | Orange | Red | Brown | Black

Grey | Pink | Purple | Light blue

White | Dark green | Light green | Silver | Gold

Other materials you will need

- Spray bottle (filled with water) to mist your paints
- Mirror
- Water pots x 2
- Glitter gel
- Glitter (cosmetic glitter ONLY; craft glitter is not for use on skin)
- Self-adhesive jewels

Techniques

Here are the basic techniques and tips for painting faces.

Sponge techniques

Laying a base

Start by spraying your paint with water using your spray bottle. Don't wet your sponge as this will cause the paint to streak, creating an uneven base.

Rub the rounded side of your sponge onto the paint.

Always add the lighter colour of your design first. Gently pat the sponge onto the skin as dragging will create streaks.

Blending

Take a second colour and load up the other side of your sponge. Gently pat this colour over the first colour. Then, turn the sponge back to the first colour. Pat on where the two colours meet to create a flawless blend of colour.

Double loading a sponge

You can load both ends of your sponge at once with two different colours. When you lay your sponge on the skin, you can 'rock' the two ends from side to side on one spot to create a blended effect quickly and easily.

Brush techniques

Here are the basic brush techniques. Try practising these strokes before painting full faces. You could practise on paper first.

Teardrops

Lay the brush flat onto the skin, then start to lift as you drag downwards and end with a flick.

Comma strokes

Lay the brush down flat, then curve the brush as you lift and drag, and end with a flick.

Tiger stripes

Start by lightly pressing the brush on the skin. Add pressure while dragging down, give a little wiggle and then release pressure, ending on a point.

Dots

The secret to dots is a good blob of wet paint on the end of a round brush. Applying different pressures creates dots of different sizes.

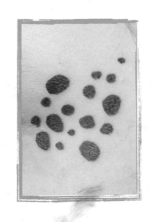

Petals

Load the brush to the metal band with paint. Lay the brush down, pressing down all the way to the end of the brush to create the perfect petal.

Double-loaded petals

Load the brush to the metal band with paint. Dip the brush tip into another colour. Press the whole brush down for two-colour petals!

Swirls and curls

Press the brush very lightly on the skin. Curve upwards and increase the pressure. As you continue round the curve, release the pressure and end on a point.

Butterfly blue

A beautiful butterfly in shades of blue flutters on the face.

1 Rub the sponge in light blue paint. Over closed eyelids, add triangles under the eyes and up to the temples.

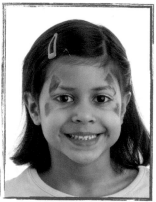

2 Add dark blue tips to the wings with the edge of the sponge. The bottom tips should be level with the nose. Blend into the light blue.

3 Outline the wings with a no. 4 brush and black paint. Add a central body and antennae.

4 Paint dark blue flowers and dots above and below opposite wings. Dot white on each wing.

YOU WILL NEED

Paints:

....

Baby sponge

....

No. 4 round paintbrush

Pink butterfly

This bright, colourful butterfly is pretty in blended purple and pink.

1 Sponge in pink triangles above and under closed eyes. Start from the corner of each eye.

2 Using purple paint on the edge of a sponge, blend from the outer edges of the wings into the pink.

3 Outline the wings in black. With a no. 4 brush, vary the pressure to paint thin to thick lines. Stop halfway under each eye.

4 Paint a black body and antennae. Add dots under the eyes to the outline. Inside the wings, add curved lines and white dots.

Side butterfly

Perched side-on, this butterfly in contrasting colours of red and yellow catches the eye.

1 Sponge on a small yellow triangle above and below one closed eye. Add an extra, thinner triangle next to the top triangle for the folded wing.

2 With red paint and a large filbert brush, add red to the outer edges of the wings.

3 Dip a no. 4 round brush in black paint and outline the wings with a scalloped (curved) design.

4 Using the no. 4 brush and black paint, add extra scalloped lines to the wings where the two colours meet. Paint small dots below the corner of the eye. Add the butterfly's body and antennae.

5 Add white dots for extra detail inside the wings. For extra colour, paint the lips red.

TOP TIP

ADD A SPRINKLE OF **GLITTER** TO THE WINGS.

Slimy snake

Hiss! A fearsome snake slithers around, showing its red tongue and sharp, white fangs.

YOU WILL NEED

Paints:

....

½ inch flat brush

....

No. 6 round paintbrush

....

No. 2 round paintbrush

1 Coat a ½ inch flat brush with light green paint and brush a thick, swirly shape on the face, from the forehead to the bottom lip.

2 Using a no. 6 brush, paint over one side of the light green swirl with dark green paint. Then create the snake's head under the nose and on the lips. Leave spaces for the snake's eyes.

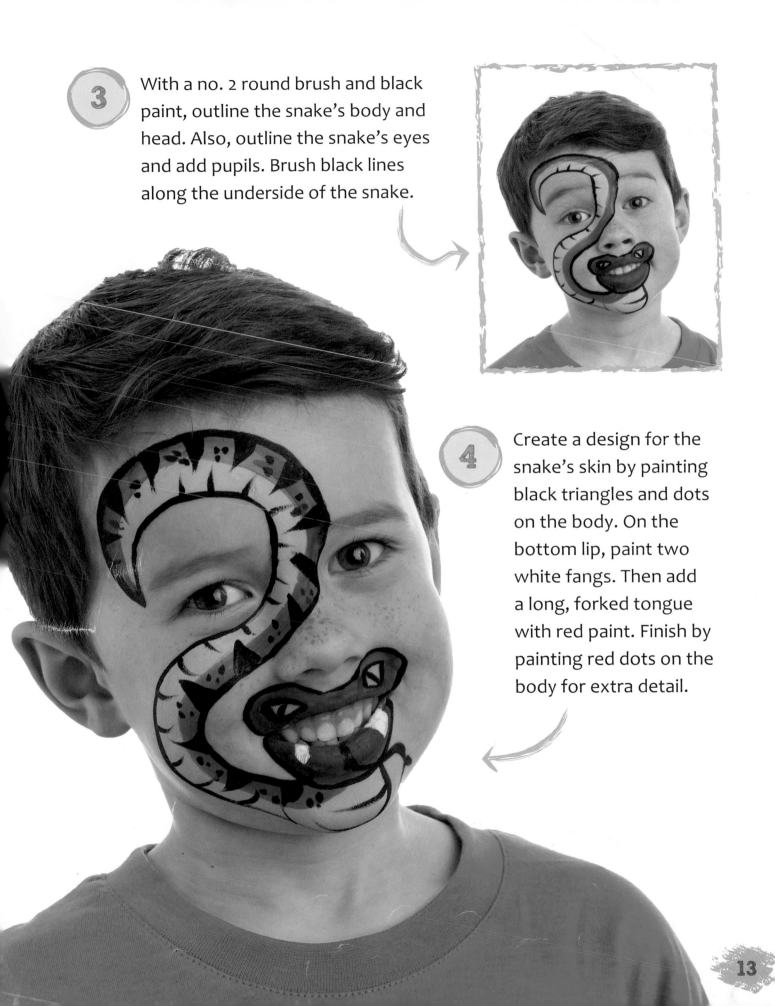

3 With a no. 2 round brush and black paint, outline the snake's body and head. Also, outline the snake's eyes and add pupils. Brush black lines along the underside of the snake.

4 Create a design for the snake's skin by painting black triangles and dots on the body. On the bottom lip, paint two white fangs. Then add a long, forked tongue with red paint. Finish by painting red dots on the body for extra detail.

13

Cute bunny

Hop into Easter as a white bunny, with an adorable pink nose and goofy teeth.

1 Use a baby sponge to shape a muzzle (mouth) in white paint up from the top lip, over the nose.

2 With a round dauber and pink paint, sponge on rosy, round cheeks under the eyes.

3 Using a no. 4 brush and black paint, lightly outline the white areas, giving the bunny a tuft of hair between the eyes, at the top of the nose. Add a small triangle nose in pink paint with a no. 4 brush. Then use a ½ inch brush and white paint to add a block for teeth over the bottom lip.

14

4 Dip a no. 4 brush in black paint to outline the bottom of the pink nose. Brush a white line on the side of the nose. Add a black line under the nose to the top lip. Add black and white whiskers. Paint the lips pink and outline the teeth in black.

One step further

At step 1, sponge white paint around the top of each eye to create a folded ear shape. At step 2, add little pink patches with the dauber to both ears. At step 3, outline the ears in black.

TOP TIP

FOR FUN, ADD A **CARROT FINGER!** PAINT ONE FINGER ORANGE AND ADD GREEN LEAVES TO THE KNUCKLE TO MAKE A CARROT TO CHEW!

15

Pirate captain

Shiver me timbers! Beware sailing the high seas when this pirate's ship is on the horizon.

1 Use a baby sponge and pink paint to create rosy cheeks. Continue over the brow bone.

2 Take a stipple sponge loaded with black paint and pat on 'stubble' around the jawline and chin.

3 Load a no. 6 brush with black paint and add a moustache and goatee beard. Paint thick, bushy eyebrows over the real eyebrows.

4 Add some hanging beads of varying sizes in red and yellow using a no. 4 brush. To make larger round beads you can use a small, round sponge dauber.

5 With a no. 6 brush and watered-down black paint, carefully outline the eyes to create a smudged eyeliner effect. Add white highlights to the beads and half outline them with watered-down black for a pale shadow.

Finally, add a cheek scar by painting an uneven line using red paint and crossing it with black lines (for stitches).

Close-up of scar

Butterfly sun

Paint a tropical butterfly. Palm trees sway, silhouetted on a sky of yellows and reds.

 1 Using a baby sponge, paint small yellow triangles over closed eyelids and the brow bone, and under the eyes.

Daubing technique

2 With red paint on the edge of a baby sponge, add red to the edges of the design and blend with the yellow.

Load your round dauber with yellow paint, then press one side into red paint. Dab onto the centre of the forehead and twist. This creates a sun.

18

3 Dip a no. 4 brush into black paint. First, make two swirls, of varying heights, that will be the palm tree trunks. Outline the edges of the design with a mixture of scalloped curves and teardrops.

4 Using a no. 2 brush and black paint, add the branches of the palm trees, falling over the sun.

5 Add leaves to the branches with a no. 2 brush and black paint. Then paint white highlights and dots to the outer edges of the design.

TOP TIP

TRY ADDING **GLITTER** TO THE EDGES.

Young pup

Yap! A red tongue and floppy ears are perfect for a cheeky puppy face.

YOU WILL NEED

Paints:

....

Baby sponge

....

No. 6 round paintbrush

....

No. 4 round paintbrush

1 With white paint, sponge a circle around the muzzle (mouth) area, going over the nose and down to the top lip. Add a little patch of white above each eye.

2 Using a no. 6 brush and brown paint, paint the folded ear shape over each eyebrow. Add a red tongue, starting on the bottom lip and going out over the chin.

3 Paint a black nose with a no. 4 brush. Add a thick line from the nose to the lip and dots to the muzzle. Colour the lips black and outline the muzzle and ears. Finally, add spots on the cheeks.

Happy dog

YOU WILL NEED

Paints:
....
Baby sponge
....
No. 4 round paintbrush
....
No. 2 round paintbrush

Woof! Paint a gentle and friendly dog face with long **whiskers** in two colours.

1 Sponge white paint down the centre of the face, from the forehead down the nose to the lips.

2 Sponge brown paint on both sides of the face to either side of the white area down to the mouth. Paint a red tongue on the bottom lip.

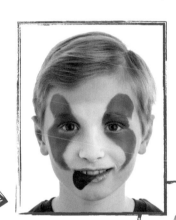

3 Using a no. 4 brush and black paint, outline the white muzzle and brown areas, drawing in the ear shapes.

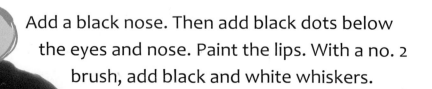

4 Add a black nose. Then add black dots below the eyes and nose. Paint the lips. With a no. 2 brush, add black and white whiskers.

21

Kitty cat

Miaow! This playful **blue and white** cat has an adorable heart-shaped nose.

1 Sponge white pointed triangles above the eyes. Then sponge white down the nose and under the nose to paint the muzzle (mouth).

2 With light blue paint, sponge the cheeks under the eyes, taking care not to go over the white. Then sponge small sides on the inner ears, above the eyebrows.

3 Outline the ear triangles with a no. 4 round brush and black paint. Then outline the muzzle, extending the lines up to the corners of the eyes. When you outline the sides of the design, use a slight zig-zag effect for fur.

4 Dip a no. 4 brush in pink paint and paint on a nose in a heart shape. Paint the lips blue and then dab on glitter.

5 Use a no. 2 brush to add whiskers – paint black and white lines. Flick the whiskers outside the muzzle. With black, add dots in the muzzle and at the top of the nose. Add a thick black line under the nose.

TOP TIP

ADD A SMALL PINK **TONGUE** ON THE BOTTOM LIP.

Fire dragon

Whoosh! A fiery dragon takes flight. White paint highlights the outstretched wings.

YOU WILL NEED

Paints:

....

½ inch flat brush

....

No. 4 round paintbrush

1 Load a ½ inch flat brush with orange paint. Create wing shapes above and below each eye. Add a scalloped edge to the wings.

2 Using a no. 4 brush and orange paint, draw the shape of a dragon's head in the centre of the forehead. Take the tail down the nose and curve round onto the cheek.

3 With the no. 4 brush and red paint, outline the wings, bringing the lines in at each scalloped edge. Outline the top of the dragon's head, body and forked tail.

4 Using a no. 4 brush and black paint, outline the wings again. Add details to the dragon – nostrils and an eye, dots to the wings, spikes on the head and curved lines to the underside of the body.

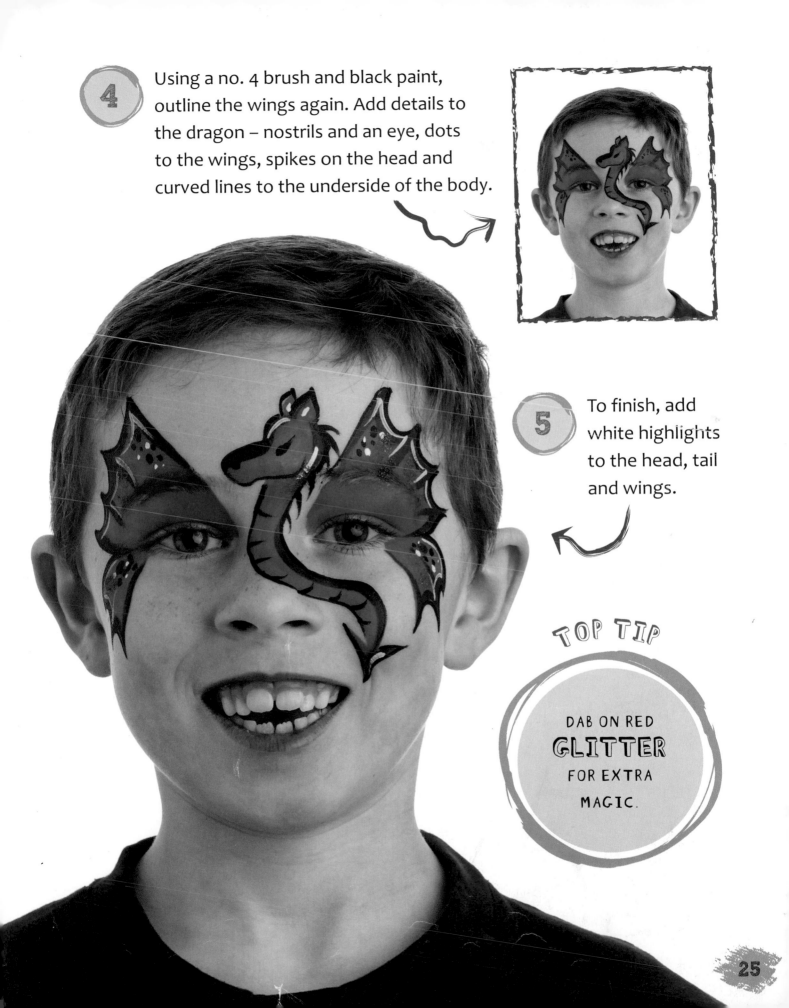

5 To finish, add white highlights to the head, tail and wings.

TOP TIP

DAB ON RED **GLITTER** FOR EXTRA MAGIC.

Dolphin splash

Splish, splash! Two watery dolphins splash and **swim** around the eyes.

1 With a no. 6 brush and light blue paint, create two droplet shapes – one above the right eye and one below the left eye.

2 Add a small dolphin nose on each shape, then add a fin and tail.

3 Create water splashes in dark blue, by painting teardrops at the end of each tail with a no. 6 brush. Add dark blue dots around the dolphins.

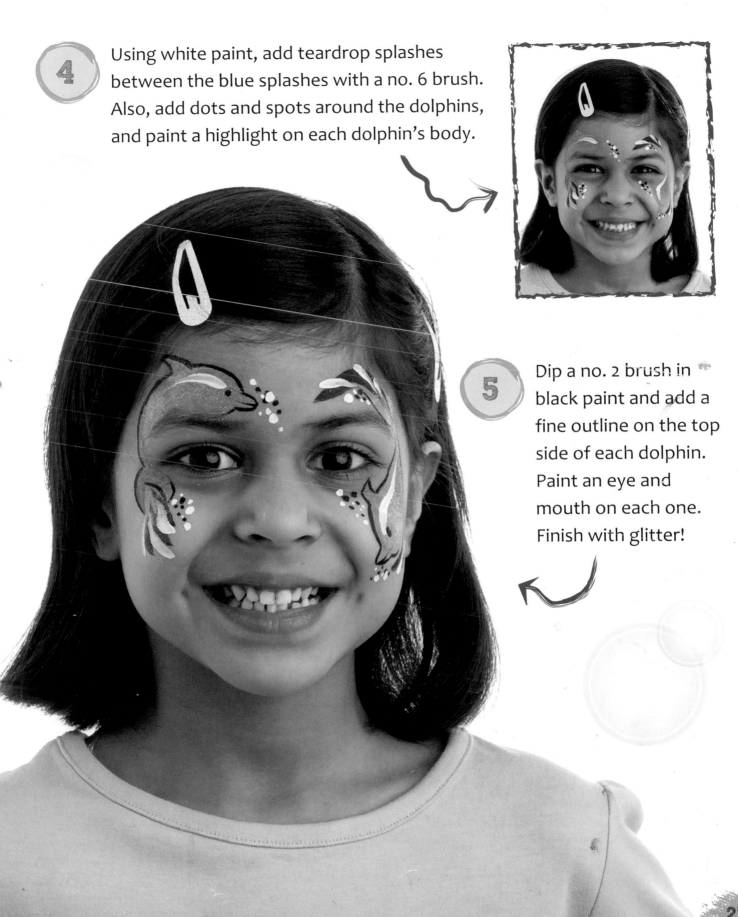

4 Using white paint, add teardrop splashes between the blue splashes with a no. 6 brush. Also, add dots and spots around the dolphins, and paint a highlight on each dolphin's body.

5 Dip a no. 2 brush in black paint and add a fine outline on the top side of each dolphin. Paint an eye and mouth on each one. Finish with glitter!

27

Tiger time

Roar! This bright, bold tiger with curved black stripes is a fierce jungle cat.

1 With white paint, sponge a triangle above each eye. Sponge white between the nose and top lip. This will be the muzzle (mouth).

2 Using yellow paint, sponge over the centre of the face, leaving space at the outer edges for the next colour.

3 Sponge orange paint around the outer edge of the face. Take care not to paint over the white areas. Blend the orange into the yellow centre. Dab orange on the tip of the nose.

4 Add tiger stripes with a no. 4 brush and black paint. First outline the white eye areas and the muzzle. Then add several more stripes. See page 7 for the stripes technique.

See page 7 for the stripes technique.

TOP TIP

YOUR DESIGN WILL LOOK BETTER IF ALL YOUR STRIPES POINT TOWARDS A **'FOCAL POINT'** BETWEEN THE EYES.

5 In black, add a nose. Paint dots on the muzzle area and in corners of the eyes. Draw a line from bottom of the nose to the top lip. Add small fangs at corners of the mouth. Paint the bottom lip orange.

Scary vampire

This spooky Halloween face is scary enough to frighten even the shadows away.

1 Using white paint, sponge a smooth, white base all over the face. Then use the edge of a sponge to add grey paint contours and shadows to the cheekbones, forehead, smile lines and eye sockets.

2 With a no. 6 brush and black paint, add spiky-shaped bushy eyebrows by sloping them down towards the inner corner of the eyes.

3 Add a triangle shape (with a jagged edge) from the centre of the forehead to the hairline. Paint black lines for cheekbones.

4 Colour in the lips with red paint. Then add small fangs at the corners of the lips, outlining them in black with a no. 2 brush.

5 With a no. 2 brush, add black nostril lines and dots next to the eyes. Paint white highlights in the black hairline triangle. Add red drips of blood coming down from the fangs.

TOP TIP

GENTLY PAT A **STIPPLE SPONGE** LOADED IN RED AT THE SIDES OF THE MOUTH FOR ADDED TEXTURE AND GORE.

Pink princess

Pretty in pink! This princess is ready to sparkle, with **swirls**, curls, teardrops and glitter.

YOU WILL NEED

Paints:

Baby sponge

½ inch flat brush

No. 4 round paintbrush

Glitter and self-adhesive jewels

1 Sponge purple paint onto both eyelids in small wing shapes.

2 Load a ½ inch flat brush with pink paint and create a pointed petal shape in the centre of the forehead. Repeat this shape on either side at a slight angle.

3 Lay the ½ inch flat brush at a 45 degree angle – press down and release as you draw the brush up towards the temples. Add little flicks at the outer corners of the eyes.

4 With a no. 4 brush and blue paint, create teardrops in the centre of the design. Start with the middle one then add two more on either side, all pointing towards the centre. Paint curls and swirls above each eye and trailing down the cheeks.

5 Using a no. 4 brush, dot pink paint in the corners of the eyes and over the coloured swirls. Add white teardrops, dots and swirls. Sprinkle with glitter and stick on a jewel or two.

One step further

Paint the lips pink and dab glitter on the bottom lip for extra sparkle.

Dinosaur roar

Keep your distance! A roaring dinosaur is on the loose. It has sharp teeth and terrible claws.

YOU WILL NEED

Paints:

No. 6 round paintbrush

No. 2 round paintbrush

 1 Dip a no. 6 brush in light green paint and start painting from the lips to make a dinosaur head and body. Take the body of the dinosaur up the cheekbone, with its tail curling around the eye.

 **2** Paint around the outer edge of your dinosaur in dark green paint with the no. 6 brush.

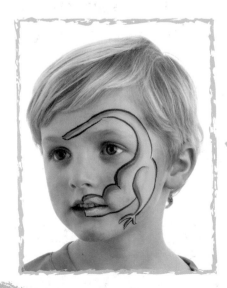

 3 Using a no. 2 brush and black paint, outline carefully around the edge of the design.

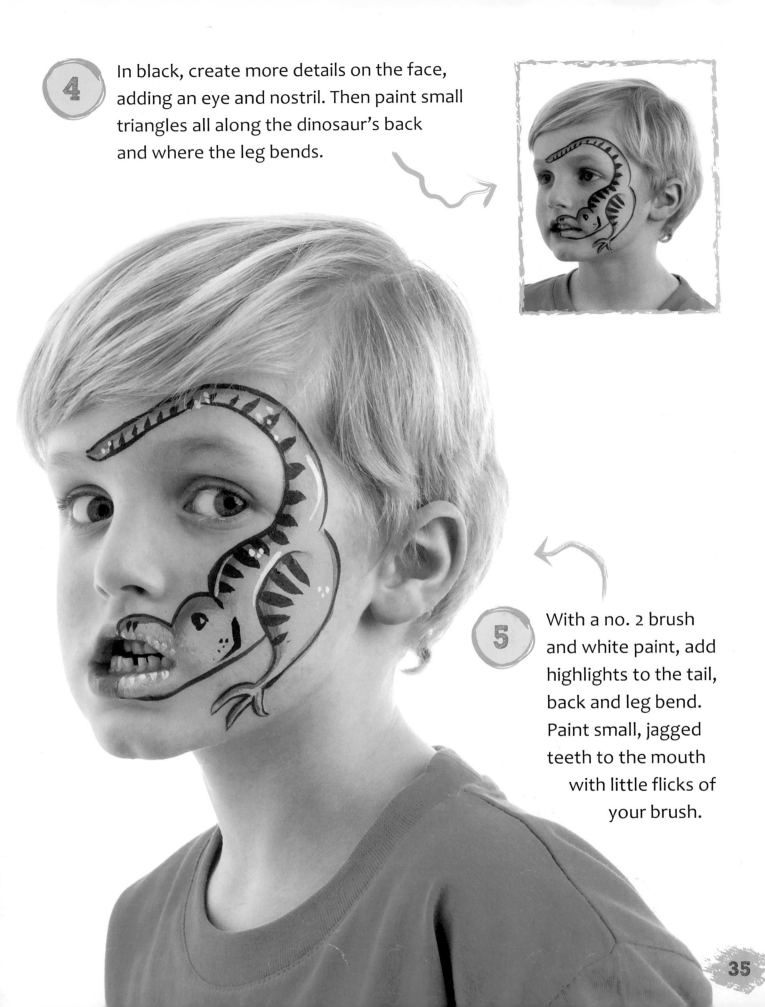

4 In black, create more details on the face, adding an eye and nostril. Then paint small triangles all along the dinosaur's back and where the leg bends.

5 With a no. 2 brush and white paint, add highlights to the tail, back and leg bend. Paint small, jagged teeth to the mouth with little flicks of your brush.

Petal rainbow

Paint a rainbow of colours and flowers around the eyes to cheer up a rainy day.

1 With a no. 6 brush and red paint, create a curved design over the forehead, coming in to the outer corners of the eyes and ending on the cheeks. Follow this red line closely with a yellow line below.

2 Paint a thinner green line below the yellow line. Then add an even thinner blue line below the green.

3 Load a petal brush with white, then double dip the tip into red paint (see page 7). Create flowers at the bends of the rainbow, and at the corner of each eye.

4 Add dots to the centre of the flowers using a no. 4 brush and white paint. Paint more dots in red near the flowers and at the inner corners of the eyes.

TOP TIP

PAINT THE LIPS
GOLD
AND ADD
GLITTER.

Prowling lion

On the savannah, a lion is on the prowl. It's a top cat that likes to steal the show.

YOU WILL NEED

Paints:

Baby sponge

No. 6 round paintbrush

No. 4 round paintbrush

1 Sponge white triangles over the corner of the eyes and under the nose, as a muzzle (mouth).

2 Using yellow paint, sponge onto the centre of the face, taking care not to go over the white paint.

3 With orange paint, sponge over the gaps on the outer edges of the design, again taking care not to go over the white. Blend the orange and yellow together.

4 Load a no. 6 brush with brown paint and create the mane. Use thick brushstrokes coming down the centre of the forehead and around the sides of the face.

5 Add a nose and outline the muzzle with a no. 4 brush and brown paint. Paint whisker lines inside the muzzle. Add black lines and white lines to the mane, and add small, white whiskers. The lips can be brown or gold.

Zombie attack

Create a masterpiece of horror. This ghoulish face has scary teeth and gory blood spurts.

YOU WILL NEED

Paints: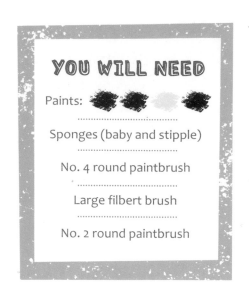

Sponges (baby and stipple)

No. 4 round paintbrush

Large filbert brush

No. 2 round paintbrush

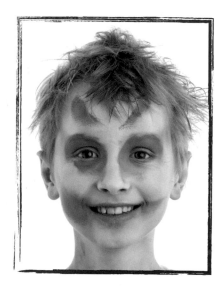

 **1** Roughly sponge a light, white base over the face, neck and ears. Using brown paint (watered down so it is lighter) and a sponge, dab lightly over the mouth, eyes, forehead and the sides of the nose. Paint messily!

2 With a no. 4 brush and unwatered brown paint, create 'angry' eyes. Drag the brown into the lighter brown. Shade in cheekbones and forehead. Add nostrils and paint an open mouth on one side.

 **3** Load a stipple sponge with red paint and dab randomly over the temples, cheekbones, mouth and neck for texture.

4 Using a no. 4 brush with red paint, add drips of blood coming from the eyes and mouth.

5 Press down a large filbert brush loaded with white to make teeth. Dip a no. 2 brush in black and outline the teeth, cheekbones, forehead and eyebrows.

One step further

Add red and brown scuffs to the knuckles.

Flower power

A summery garland of colourful flowers decorates one eye in this effective design.

1 Start by sponging a curved shape in pink around one eye, going over the closed eyelid.

Flower close-up

2 With a no. 4 brush and red paint, press down your brush to create petals, moving your brush around in a circle. Paint three flowers spaced out.

3 Fully load a petal brush with white paint. Press down the brush to make two more flowers between the red flowers.

4 Using a no. 4 brush with green paint, add leaves between each flower by making small flicks with the brush, ending on a point.

5 Add dots in the centre of the flowers using a no. 4 brush and purple paint. Fill any remaining space with more purple dots.

TOP TIP

PAINT
THE LIPS
RED.

Flower fairy

Add flowery magic with coloured petals, curls and swirls. A design for fairies of the garden.

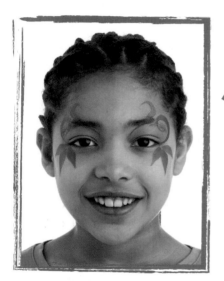

1 Sponge a pink triangle over closed eyelids. With a no. 4 brush, add green leaves below the eyes and swirls above the eyes.

2 Load a petal brush with white paint. Dip the tip into purple paint. Press down the brush and make a five-petal flower with trailing petals (see page 7, 'double-loaded petals').

3 With a no. 4 brush and purple paint, add more swirls and curls above the eyes, tangling with the leaves.

4 Using a no. 4 brush, add white dots to the centre of the flower and around the petals. Outline the purple swirls in white.

One step further

Create a garland of petals. Sponge light blue over the eyelids and brow. Paint dark blue teardrops with a no. 4 brush to make three flowers. Load a petal brush with white, double dip into dark blue and add a flower above each eye. Add green leaves and blue wavy lines.

Bat mask

Swoop! Black bats fly in a sunset sky. One large bat forms a perfect mask shape.

1 Start with yellow paint and sponge a half circle above the eyes and over closed eyelids. Sponge down the centre of the nose.

2 Dip a no. 6 brush in orange paint and paint a crescent shape in the centre of the forehead. Blend the orange into the yellow by dabbing with the edge of the sponge.

3 Paint a small circle between the eyes using a no. 4 brush and black paint. Add pointed ears and a pointed body.

4 With a no. 4 brush and black paint, add wings, curving up around the yellow and orange half-circle. Curve the wings down around the eyes to a point. Finish level with the nose. With a dry sponge, drag black paint down over the eyelids into the yellow.

5 Draw small flying bats in the sunset with a no. 4 brush and black paint. Add an extra flick to both wings. Dab on a moon using white paint on a small sponge dauber. Then paint white and black starbursts and dots in the orange sky. Add black dots below each eye.

Swirly fairy

This fairy has sparkle and style – teardrops, dots, swirls and curls... and a dash of glitter.

 1 Sponge a pink triangle above and below each eye, over closed eyelids and brow.

 **2** With purple paint, sponge around the pink, and dab onto the centre of the forehead. Blend the purple into the pink.

 3 Outline the design with white swirls, curls and teardrops (see page 7) using a no. 4 brush.

4 Dip a no. 4 brush ~~dark~~ blue paint. Add teardrops and dots between the white patterns.

5 Load a no. 2 brush with white paint and add dots and starbursts. Paint the lips pink and dab glitter on the lips and above the eyes. Finish by sticking on fairy jewels!

Monster mask

Run! There's a scary monster on the loose. It has horns, fangs and scales!

 1 Sponge green paint over and above closed eyelids, down the nose and onto the cheeks in a mask shape.

2 Using a darker green and the edge of a sponge, add shadows over the eyes and at the top and bottom of the mask.

 3 With a no. 4 round brush and white paint, add pointed horns and fangs at the top and bottom of the mask.

4 Load a no. 2 brush with black paint and add nostrils. Using the 'thin to thick technique' (see 'tiger stripes' on page 7), outline the mask with a wiggly line and add eyebrows. Outline the horns and fangs, adding tiny vertical lines at the bases of each one.

5 Using a large filbert brush, add scales to the cheeks and down the nose. Load one side of the brush with light green. Then load the other side with dark green. Lay the brush with the light green facing down and press. Lift the brush to reveal a 'U'-shaped scale.

Scales technique

Great giraffe

Stand tall and reach for the treetops! This giraffe has hair, horns and brown patches.

YOU WILL NEED

Paints:

....

Baby sponge

....

No. 6 round paintbrush

....

No. 4 round paintbrush

1 With yellow paint, sponge on a giraffe-shaped face over closed eyelids. Leave a gap between the eyes for a patch of hair.

2 Using orange paint, sponge around the edges, blending the orange into the yellow.

3 Add a patch of hair between the eyes with a no. 6 round brush and white paint. Draw a few strokes of white hair in the centre of the ears.

4 Using a no. 4 brush and brown paint, outline the face, hair and ears. Add small horns beside each ear and a tuft detail to the outer corner of each eye.

TOP TIP

MAKE THE
MARKINGS
SYMMETRICAL.

5 Dip a no. 6 brush in brown paint and add giraffe markings down the cheeks. Paint nostrils on the sides of the nose and fill the lips in brown. Finish with dots in the corners of the eyes.

Snow queen

Whoosh! A glittery, icy snow queen whirls into view in a flurry of snowflakes.

1 Sponge two light blue triangles over each closed eyelid to the temple, and a circle of blue in the centre of the forehead.

2 Using a no. 6 brush and dark blue paint, outline the triangles with swirly lines, curling at the top. Create a curl from the outer corner of each eye over the light blue paint. Then add teardrops (see page 7) below it.

3 Create a six-pointed snowflake in the centre of the forehead with a no. 4 brush and white paint. Add small flicks to each point of the snowflake. Paint smaller starbursts in white over the cheeks and forehead.

 4 With a no. 4 brush and white paint, add extra teardrops beside the snowflake and small, white dots on the cheeks and forehead.

5 Still using a no. 6 brush, fill in the lips with blue paint. Add glitter to the bottom lip.

TOP TIP

STICK A SHINY **JEWEL** ON THE CENTRE OF THE SNOWFLAKE.

Space robot

Beep! Zoom into the future with this **silver-panelled** robot from outer space.

YOU WILL NEED

Paints:
....
Baby sponge
....
No. 2 round paintbrush
....
½ inch flat brush
....
Glitter

1 Cover the entire face in silver paint using a sponge. Close the eyes to paint the eyelids. Then add shapes in dark blue on the forehead and chin with a no. 2 brush.

2 Outline the blue areas with thin black lines using a no. 2 brush. To make the face panels, add extra lines down the sides of nose, around the mouth and above the eyebrows. Outline the whole face.

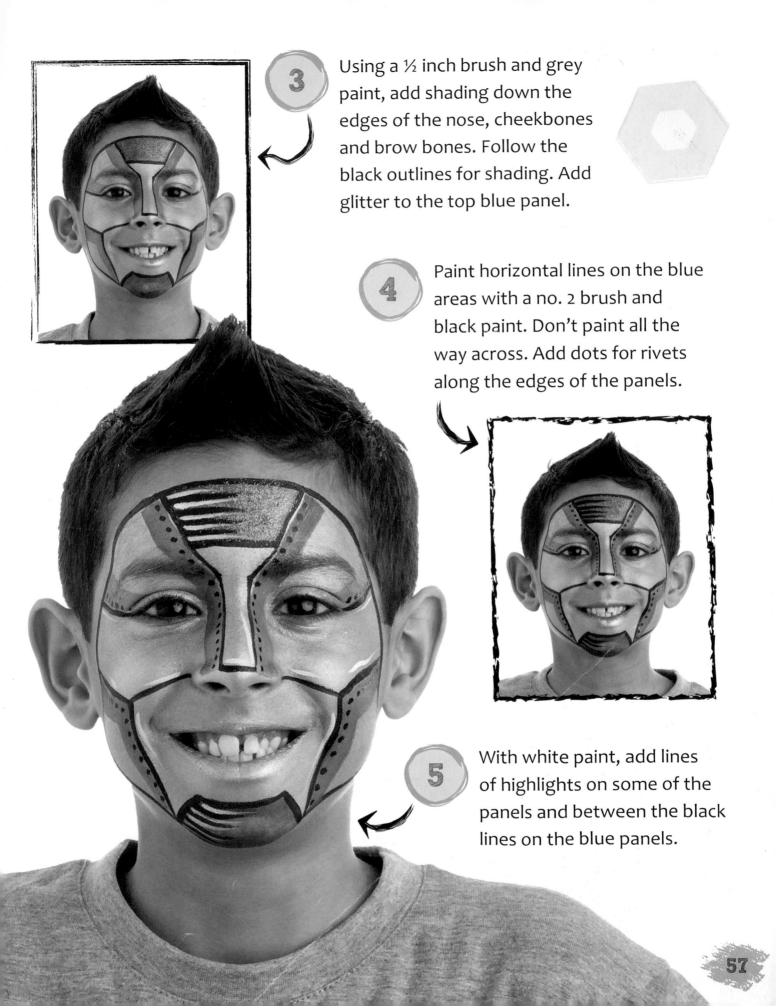

3 Using a ½ inch brush and grey paint, add shading down the edges of the nose, cheekbones and brow bones. Follow the black outlines for shading. Add glitter to the top blue panel.

4 Paint horizontal lines on the blue areas with a no. 2 brush and black paint. Don't paint all the way across. Add dots for rivets along the edges of the panels.

5 With white paint, add lines of highlights on some of the panels and between the black lines on the blue panels.

Spooky skull

Transform a happy face into an angry, sinister skull with white, black and grey paint.

1 With white paint, sponge a smooth, white base over the whole face. Close the eyes when sponging over them.

2 Load the edge of a sponge with grey paint. Add shadows to the eye sockets, forehead and cheekbones, dragging down to the jawline. When the sponge is almost dry, dab lightly over the lips with grey.

3 To look angry, outline the eye sockets with a no. 4 round brush and black paint. Take the paint down to the inner corners of the eyes and add lines at either side of the nose. Using a sponge, drag the black paint into the grey. Add a triangle on either side of the nose.

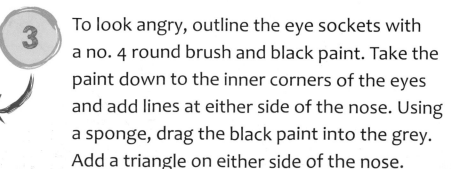

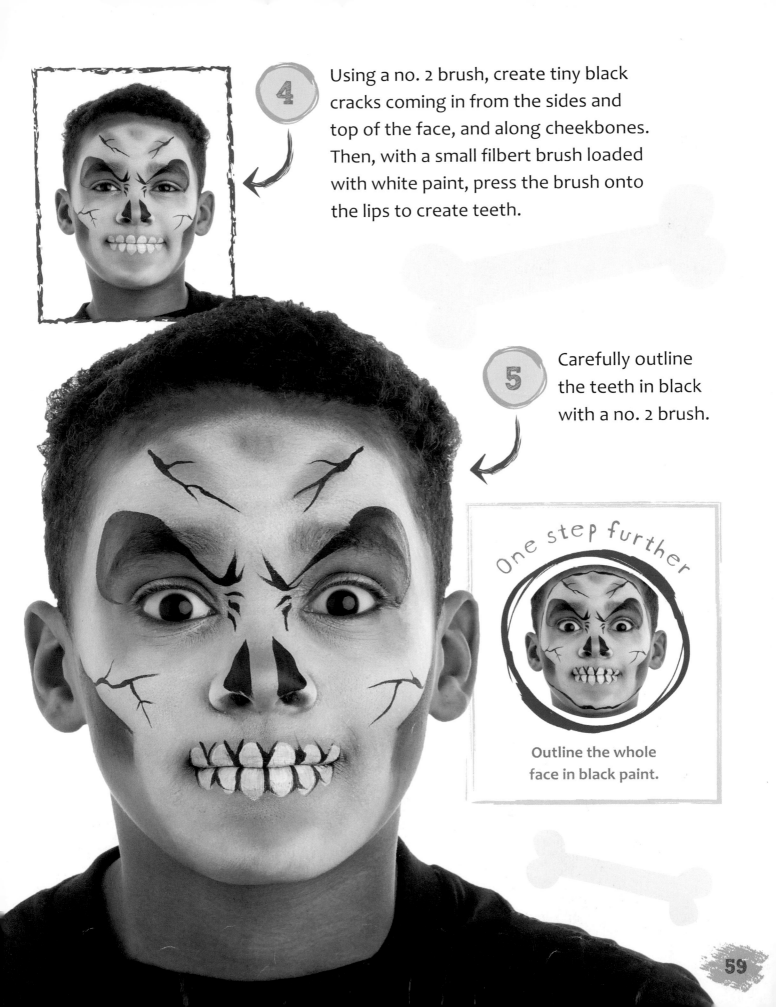

4 Using a no. 2 brush, create tiny black cracks coming in from the sides and top of the face, and along cheekbones. Then, with a small filbert brush loaded with white paint, press the brush onto the lips to create teeth.

5 Carefully outline the teeth in black with a no. 2 brush.

One step further

Outline the whole face in black paint.

Wicked witch

Covered with cobwebs and warts, this green-skinned witch might cast a spell or two.

YOU WILL NEED

Paints:

Baby sponge

No. 2 round paintbrush

No. 3 round paintbrush

1 Start by sponging the whole face with light green paint. Close the eyes when sponging over them.

2 Load the edge of the sponge with dark green paint and add contours and shadows to the chin, cheekbones, temples, eyes and smile lines. With a no. 2 brush, lightly paint bags and wrinkles under the eyes.

3 Draw a large cobweb on the forehead using a no. 2 brush and black paint.

4 With a no. 4 brush and black paint, create angry eyes by painting arched eyebrows coming right to the corners of the eyes. Add dots and wrinkles at the bridge of the nose. When the paint on the brush is almost dry, add lines at the bottom of the nose and cheeks.

5 Staying with the no. 4 brush, colour in the lips black. To paint warts, add white dots outlined in black with a no. 2 brush. Paint fine hairs coming out of them. Vary the size of the warts and add them wherever you like.

Close-up of wart

Merry deer

It's Christmas! Here comes jolly Rudolph with a red nose and holly berries on his brow.

YOU WILL NEED

Paints:

....
Baby sponge
....
No. 4 round paintbrush
....
Red glitter

1 Sponge white paint around the muzzle (mouth) and chin. Add small triangles over closed eyelids to create ears.

2 Mix the brown paint with some red and a little white. Sponge the reddy-brown mixture around the white ears, and across the cheeks, down to the muzzle.

3 With unmixed brown, outline the design using a no. 4 brush. Add a sloping brown line inside each ear. Outline the white muzzle and paint a thick line from the nose to the top lip. Add antlers to the forehead.

4 Paint holly below the antlers – see 'One step further' (below) for instructions. Add a red nose.

5 Add big, white dots to the cheeks, and a small, white highlight on the nose and holly. Paint short, white whiskers, then add brown dots on the muzzle. To finish, paint the bottom lip brown.

One step further

Using a no. 4 brush and light green paint, paint holly leaves from the corners of the eyes. Use dark green to outline and shade the leaves. Add red berries (dots). Paint a white line in the centre of the leaves and white dots in and by each berry. This simple, striking design works well on its own.

TOP TIP

FOR EXTRA SPARKLE, ADD RED **GLITTER** TO THE ROSY NOSE!

Index

Online suppliers

The following websites are recommended suppliers in the UK:

www.thefacepaintingshop.com
www.funtimefaces.co.uk
www.facepaint-uk.com
http://illusionmagazine.co.uk
www.facepaintsdirect.co.uk
http://facadebodyart.co.uk